W9-BJT-824

Matter

by Jane Weir

Science Contributor
Sally Ride Science

Science Consultant
Michael E. Kopecky, Science Educator

MISSION: SCIENCE

Sally Ride
Science

Sally Ride Science™ is an innovative content company dedicated to fueling young people's interests in science.

Our publications and programs provide opportunities for students and teachers to explore the captivating world of science—from astrobiology to zoology.

We bring science to life and show young people that science is creative, collaborative, fascinating, and fun.

To learn more, visit www.SallyRideScience.com

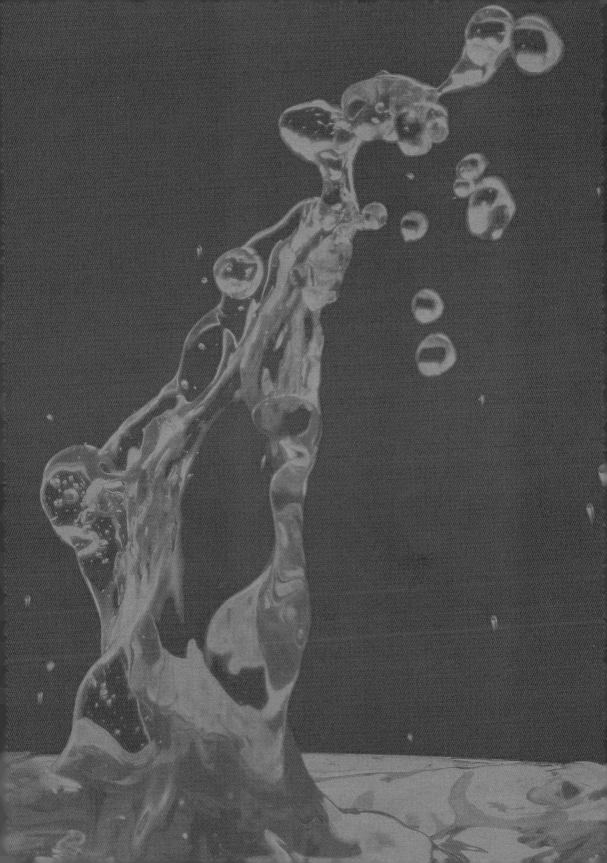

First hardcover edition published in 2009 by
Compass Point Books
151 Good Counsel Drive
P.O. Box 669
Mankato, MN 56002-0669

Editor: Jennifer VanVoorst
Designer: Heidi Thompson
Editorial Contributor: Sue Vander Hook

Art Director: LuAnn Ascheman-Adams
Creative Director: Joe Ewest
Editorial Director: Nick Healy
Managing Editor: Catherine Neitge

 This book was manufactured with paper containing at least 10 percent post-consumer waste.

Library of Congress Cataloging-in-Publication Data
Weir, Jane, 1976–
  Matter / by Jane Weir
  p. cm. — (Mission: Science)
  Includes index.
  ISBN 978-0-7565-4069-2 (library binding)
1. Matter—Juvenile literature. 2. Matter—Properties--Juvenile literature. I. Title.
  QC173.36.W453 2009
  530—dc22   2008037624

Visit Compass Point Books on the Internet at *www.compasspointbooks.com*
or e-mail your request to *custserv@compasspointbooks.com*

Table of Contents

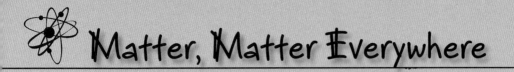

Matter, Matter Everywhere

Matter is everywhere—but just what is matter? Matter is your house and every item in it. It's your school building, books, backpack, shoes, hair, and fingernails. Matter is outside—it's dirt, grass, birds, telephone poles, and air. It's everything you can imagine on Earth, in the sky, and in our universe. Matter is everything you touch and see, and even what you can't see.

Objects of matter can be very different from each other. Some are shiny, and some are dull. Some are soft, while others are extremely hard. Matter can be magnetic or radioactive. It can be cold, hot, brittle, bouncy, solid, or squishy. It might be liquid or gas. A morsel of matter might be good to eat, or it could be poisonous. Matter is still matter, regardless of whether it's alive or dead. In fact, certain types of matter have never been alive.

By definition, matter is whatever occupies space and has mass. It is the "stuff" that makes up everything. There are billions of types of matter in our universe. But what makes up matter? Amazingly, there are only about 100 different "ingredients" that make up the billions of things in our universe. These ingredients are called elements.

Everything in the universe is made up of matter.

Elements and Atoms

Now we know that matter is made up of elements. But let's go a little further. What is an element made of? An element is composed of atoms. Atoms are very small. They are extremely tiny particles that can only be seen under a powerful microscope. Atoms are so small that it would take about 1,000 years to count all the atoms in a single dot—like the period at the end of this sentence. The number of atoms in your body couldn't be counted even if you had all the time since the universe began.

Atoms combine in many ways. Things that are made up of just one type of atom are called elements. But atoms can also combine to make a variety of matter. This combination is called atomic arrangement.

Did You Know?

There are about one septillion water molecules—connected atoms—in one medium-sized glass of water. And there are more atoms in a teaspoon of water than there are teaspoons of water in the entire Atlantic Ocean.

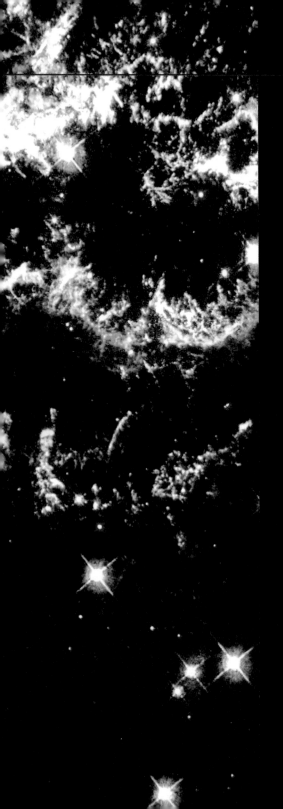

Human, Soup, or Stardust?

The universe started off as mostly the element hydrogen. All the other elements were formed in nuclear reactions in stars. When stars get old, some of them swell and explode, scattering a variety of elements all over the universe. Elements make up all the things we see on Earth, including humans. The atoms in our bodies are no different from the atoms in a can of soup or in a distant star. It is the way atoms are arranged that makes humans different from soup or stardust.

Inside Atoms

So matter is made of elements, and elements are made of atoms. But what's an atom made of? Each atom is made up of even smaller parts called protons, neutrons, and electrons. The protons and neutrons are crowded tightly together in the nucleus, in the middle of the atom. Outside the nucleus is an area of the atom that is mostly empty space. There, tiny electrons zip around the nucleus. Electrons, which are even smaller than protons or neutrons, travel at a very rapid speed.

Inside every atom is a bunch of energy, or electric charges. Protons have a positive electric charge, while electrons have a negative charge. Neutrons have no charge at all. Each atom always has the same number of protons and electrons. Their charges, positive and negative, balance each other out, which means that most atoms have no charge.

Grab an Electron

Even if it were possible to see the parts of an atom, it would be impossible to grab hold of a swift-moving electron as it whirled past. Electrons move so quickly that they appear to be everywhere at once.

Science Tip

Don't confuse atoms with cells. Cells are much bigger than atoms. In fact, cells are made of atoms.

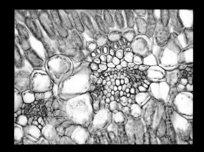

Hello, Out There!

The nucleus at the center of an atom is very tiny. The electrons circling the nucleus are very far away. To imagine this, think of the atom as a pea in the middle of a football stadium. If the pea were the nucleus, then the electrons would be whizzing around outside the stadium.

That's something like what happens when you mix equal parts of black and white paint. You no longer have black or white. Instead, you have gray—kind of a neutral color. Most atoms are neutral, too. That means they have no charge.

The thing that makes each element different from another is the number of protons and electrons in their atoms. The hydrogen atom, the simplest type of atom, has only one proton, one electron, and no neutrons.

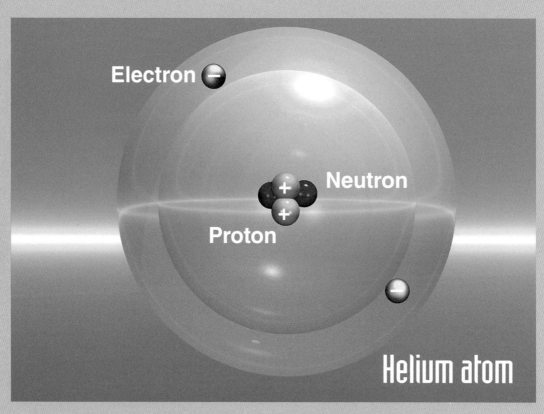

Electron

Neutron

Proton

Helium atom

▲ In a helium atom, the two positive protons balance the two negative electrons.

How Stable Are Elements?

When a substance is made up of only one kind of atom, it is called an element. Elements can't be changed into other elements. In other words, iron will always be iron. It can't be changed into gold. You can heat it. You can hit it. You can drop it in acid. But no matter what you do, it will still be iron. It might not look the same after doing these things, but it will still be composed of iron atoms.

The reason is simple. To change one element into another would mean changing the nucleus of each atom. It is very difficult to break apart a nucleus. The nucleus is held together by a very strong force.

Did You Know?

In the past, people believed they could make gold. They thought that heating common metals with other elements would transform them. Today we know this isn't true. An element can't be changed by heat or anything else.

The Periodic Table

All the elements can be grouped according to their properties, which make each element unique. Properties include such things as number of electrons and distance between atoms. Elements can also be grouped by how reactive they are—how they react with one another and how they react to heat and cold.

In 1869, Russian scientist Dmitri Mendeleev created a chart to organize the elements. It is called the periodic table of the elements. The table is still used today. When Mendeleev created the table, there were about 60 known elements. Mendeleev left blank spots and question marks on his table because he predicted that more elements would be discovered. He was right. As of 2008, the periodic table contained 117 elements.

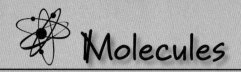
When atoms join together, they make molecules. These connected atoms share some of the whirling electrons. Molecules can then join together to form substances. Each molecule of a substance has the same properties as the whole. That means that one molecule of a substance reacts in the same way as the whole group of them.

Some elements have more than one atom. Of course, they are the same kind of atom because they are elements. Oxygen, which is in the air we breathe, is a good example. An oxygen molecule is made up of two oxygen atoms bonded together. It can be written as O_2.

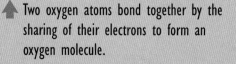

Two oxygen atoms bond together by the sharing of their electrons to form an oxygen molecule.

Why Do Snowflakes Have Six Sides?

When molecules join with one another, they do it in patterns. The patterns they make depend on how the molecules are attracted to one another. The shape of the molecules and their tiny bonds determine what patterns we see. When water freezes, each molecule makes six bonds to other water molecules. That's why snowflakes have six sides.

Compounds

What happens when two or more elements join together? They form an entirely new substance. The atoms are held together by a chemical bond. This new substance is called a compound. Let's say that two hydrogen atoms join up with one oxygen atom. In chemistry, that's written as H_2O. The number 2 means there are two hydrogen atoms. No number after the O means there is just one oxygen atom.

H_2O is a compound because two separate elements—hydrogen and oxygen—have joined together. We know this compound as water. Water has completely different properties from either hydrogen or oxygen.

Compounds are made by elements that join easily with each other. These are called reactive elements. Some elements are very reactive, and some are not. The more reactive an element is, the more likely it will be to form compounds.

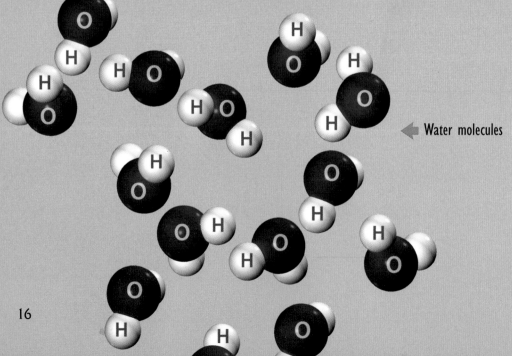

← Water molecules

Why Can I Eat Sodium Chloride but Not Sodium or Chlorine?

The chemical name for salt is sodium chloride. Each salt molecule is made up of one atom of sodium and one atom of chlorine. Scientists use abbreviations—chemical symbols from the periodic table—to show what elements are in a substance. Na is the symbol for sodium, and Cl is the symbol for chlorine. Therefore, salt is written as NaCl. On its own, sodium (Na) is a metal that you wouldn't want to eat. Chlorine (Cl) is a poisonous gas. But together, they make salt. Salt is neither a metal nor a poison. When certain elements join together, they react to the union and make a brand new substance. The new substance has properties that are completely different from the elements from which it was made. Another example is rust. The elements in rust are iron (Fe) and oxygen (O). But rust doesn't have the properties of either iron or oxygen.

Too Hot to Handle

A very unreactive element is argon gas. It is used in lightbulbs because it won't catch fire when it gets hot. A very reactive element is sodium metal. It needs to be kept in oil because if it touches air, it can catch fire.

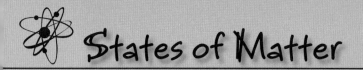

States of Matter

Matter can exist as either a liquid, a solid, or a gas. These are called states of matter. For example, when water is in its liquid state, you can swim in it, drink it, or take a shower in it. You can water plants with it or use it to fill your dog's water bowl. But when water is in its solid state, you can skate on it or put it in your drinks to make them cold. Water in this state is called ice. But it is still H_2O.

When water is a gas, it is called water vapor or steam. You can't drink water vapor, and it would never stay in your dog's water bowl. It's what you see rising into the air when water boils. It's the cloudy mist that hovers over a bowl of hot soup. Water vapor is also what clouds are made of.

Why Does Water Appear Outside My Glass?

On a hot, humid day, the air contains many water molecules. These molecules have a lot of energy and move around a great deal in the air. If they hit the sides of a cold glass, they lose some of their energy and slow down. Some of the molecules slow down so much that they don't have enough energy to float around in the air anymore. They have turned into liquid on the outside of your glass.

⬆ Clouds are a form of water vapor.

⬆ Icebergs are like ice cubes floating in a
glass of water. They float in the ocean.
Just like ice cubes, they rise to the surface.

Substances can change from one state of matter to another. For example, ice may melt, or water may evaporate. But changing the state of matter doesn't change the makeup of the molecules. Whether it's water, ice, or vapor, it's still two atoms of hydrogen combined with one atom of oxygen.

Heat has a lot to do with changing the state of matter. Heat causes molecules to move faster, vibrate more, and move away from each other. The molecules in steam are very active with a lot of distance between each other. The molecules in cold water are closer together and move around randomly at a slower pace. And when water freezes, the molecules stop moving completely and clump together. That's why you can hold an ice cube in your hand. But if you hold an ice cube long enough, the heat from your hand will melt the ice and change it back into water.

Freeze It

Most matter contracts when it freezes. This is because the molecules slow down and get closer to each other. Water, however, is different. It is one of the few substances that expands when it freezes. When a water molecule freezes, it forms a six-sided bond with the other molecules. These six projections on each molecule mean the molecules can't get as close to each other as they were as a liquid. The molecules have to move farther apart, thus taking up more space.

Try this experiment to prove that ice takes up more space than water: Put a very full container of water in the freezer with a lid on it. When the water freezes, check your container. More than likely, the lid has popped off because the ice needed more space.

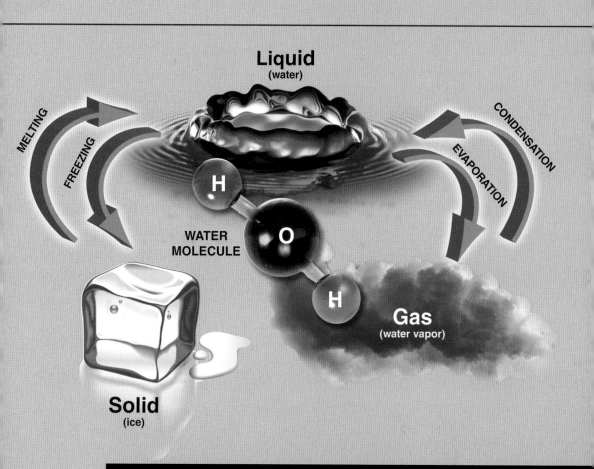

Liquid
(water)

MELTING

FREEZING

CONDENSATION

EVAPORATION

H

O

H

WATER
MOLECULE

Gas
(water vapor)

Solid
(ice)

Moving Windows

Glass is a solid, but it acts like a liquid over long periods of time. Some very old windows in buildings found in Europe are thicker at the bottom than at the top because the glass has "flowed" downward over time.

Molecules in a solid are packed together closely. They move only by vibrating in their fixed positions. That is why solids keep their shape. They don't float, and they don't flow. It's hard to compress solids because their molecules are already so close together.

Molecules in liquids are farther apart and move past each other easily. They change shape, flow, and spread out to make puddles. A liquid will fill any solid container and conform to the shape of that container.

The molecules in a gas are the freest. They keep their distance from other molecules, leaving plenty of room for them to move about. Gases will also fill up the space in a container, but you usually can't see them. Since molecules in a gas are far apart, it's easy to compress them, or push the molecules closer together. Scuba divers carry a tank of compressed air on their backs when they swim underwater. This source of air allows them to stay underwater for long periods of time.

Solid

Liquid

Gas

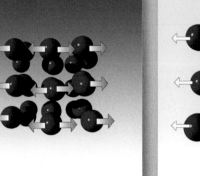
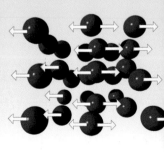

A change from a solid to a liquid or a gas is marked by a change in the space between molecules.

Why Does Soup Cool Faster When I Blow on It?

The surface of a hot bowl of soup is an active place. If you could magnify it millions of times, you would see molecules dancing all about. You would see some molecules floating upward and then coming right back down to the soup. Other molecules would escape into the air and never return. But if you were to blow on the soup, your breath would push away some of the most energetic molecules on and just above the surface. You would be left with soup with less energy—which translates to less heat. Your soup would now be cool enough to eat.

When you cool something, you take energy from it. The colder the matter is, the less energy it has, and the slower its atoms move. When temperatures drop, most matter turns to a solid. But if the temperature drops extremely low—to minus 459 degrees Fahrenheit (minus 273 degrees Celsius), called absolute zero— molecules take on a new state of matter. It is called a quantum state.

Scientists are still studying what happens to molecules at absolute zero. The molecules move ever so slightly, with something like a faint vibration. Scientists have also discovered that at this temperature a large portion of the molecules collapse and take on a new state of matter. This quantum state is when the smallest amount of energy exists.

Absolute Zero

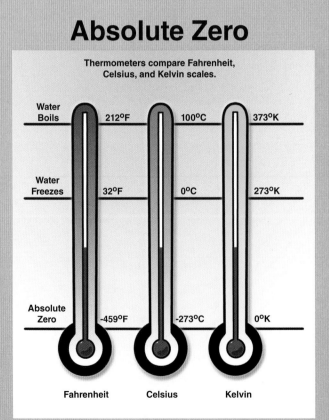

Thermometers compare Fahrenheit, Celsius, and Kelvin scales.

	Fahrenheit	Celsius	Kelvin
Water Boils	212°F	100°C	373°K
Water Freezes	32°F	0°C	273°K
Absolute Zero	-459°F	-273°C	0°K

Temperature is measured according to three scales— Fahrenheit, Celsius, and Kelvin. Absolute zero is equivalent to 0 degrees Kelvin.

Max Planck
(1858—1947)

Max Planck's teachers told him there was nothing new to learn in science. But Planck believed there was more to discover. After graduating from college, he experimented with thermodynamics, the study of heat and energy. He was especially interested in the colors of light that radiated from very hot matter. Other scientists believed that light was a continuous wave. But Planck believed that light, or energy from atoms, comes in separate packets or particles. He called them quanta. A single particle is called a quantum. His idea transformed the science of physics, the study of how matter and energy interact. His work changed the way scientists thought about light, energy, and matter. In 1919, Planck received the Nobel Prize in physics for his discovery of energy quanta.

Planck's quantum theory helped prove that light travels at a constant speed, even when the light source is moving. ⬇

Mixtures

Compounds and mixtures sound like similar things, but in chemistry, they are quite different. A compound is when two or more elements combine and hold together by a chemical bond to form a new substance. A mixture, on the other hand, is two or more substances mixed together. But there is no chemical bond. Air and blood are both mixtures. They contain a variety of substances. Since the substances in a mixture still retain their own identities, they can be separated easily—if you know how.

Separating Mixtures

Mixtures can be separated in a variety of ways. Some mixtures can be separated by using a simple filter such as a cloth or screen. The substance with the smaller particles will pass through the filter, while the substance with the larger particles will collect on top. For example, a filter can keep out solids that are found in the air. Sometimes pollen or allergens mix with the air we breathe and cause us to sneeze. A dust mask is a type of filter worn over your nose and mouth. It will let in the air but keep out the particles that make you sneeze.

Did You Know?

You can separate carbon dioxide from soda pop. If you blow air through a straw into a glass of soda pop, the bubbles will take the carbon dioxide to the top where they will escape into the air. Eventually the liquid will go "flat."

What Makes a Lava Lamp Work?

Have you ever seen a lava lamp? A brightly colored light shines on a constantly moving and changing mass inside a glass container. A lava lamp works because there is a mixture inside. The moving lump is a mixture of water and wax. Wax is denser than water when it is cold. It is nearly a solid that sits at the bottom of the lamp. But when the lamp is turned on, a heater at the bottom warms the wax and softens it. As it gets hot, the wax becomes less dense than the water. Now it can float to the top of the lamp—usually in blobs. The heat keeps the wax part of the mixture moving through the water.

27

Boiling is another way to separate substances in a mixture. For example, boiling seawater evaporates the water and leaves the salt crystals behind.

Magnets can be used to separate metals from other substances. Some breakfast cereals have tiny pieces of iron in them to increase their iron content. Try swirling a magnet through an iron-fortified cereal. The iron, a metal, will stick to the magnet.

More complex mixtures can be separated using a process called chromatography. This procedure is performed in a laboratory with special equipment. When a mixture passes through certain liquids or gases, the different parts spread out from each other and separate. Chromatography is often used to identify substances such as blood at a crime scene.

Seawater can be boiled to separate the ⬆ mixture into water vapor and salt crystals.

To separate a mixture using chromatography, a scientist places a small amount of the mixture on a piece of filter paper and then slowly drips a solvent, a substance that can dissolve another one, into the center of the paper. The solvent then spreads the mixture out at differing rates. The distance traveled over time is used to identify each component.

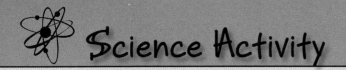

Separating Mixtures

Physicists study how matter and energy work together. They need to know what matter is made of and how it behaves. Knowing how various substances act when they are mixed together is also important. Sometimes molecules bond together chemically and form a compound. A good example is hydrogen (H) and oxygen (O), which join together to make water (H_2O). Other times, substances simply mix together but keep their own identities. What is mixed can also be unmixed. This science activity will show you how to separate substances that have been mixed together. You will need to know some laws of physics in order to do it.

Materials

- mixture of pebbles, sand, salt, and iron filings

- sieve with ½–inch (1.3-centimeter) holes

- filter paper

- filter funnel

- spoon

- 2 large beakers

- strong magnet

- tripod

- gauze

- tongs

- water

Procedure

1 Mix the pebbles, sand, salt, and iron filings.

2 Now you will separate them. In order to do this, you will need to use what you have learned about mixtures, their properties, and how to separate them. Think about what you know about the materials in the mixture. Think about their properties. How can you separate them? Follow these remaining steps:

3 Sift out the pebbles using the sieve.

4 Use the magnet to remove the iron filings.

5 Put the sand and salt mixture into the large beaker. Add water and stir until all the salt is dissolved.

6 Put the filter paper inside the filter funnel. Put a second large beaker under the funnel spout. Pour the liquid mixture through the filter in the funnel. The sand will remain in the filter paper.

7 Put the remaining liquid mixture (in the second beaker) in a very warm or hot place until all the liquid evaporates. The only thing left is the salt. The sand will remain in the filter paper.

You have successfully separated each substance from the mixture.

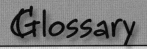

absolute zero—coldest temperature that anything can possibly get and at which all energy is removed from it

atom—smallest particle of an element; it contains protons, neutrons, and electrons, and makes up all matter

atomic arrangement—the way atoms are arranged

chromatography—process for separating mixtures of substances with different boiling points or solubility

compound—substance made up of two or more different types of atoms joined together by chemical bonds

electron—small particle with a negative charge that travels fast around an atom

element—substance that is composed of just one type of atom and cannot be reduced to simpler substances by normal chemical means

evaporate—change from a liquid state of matter to a gas

matter—something that has mass and exists as a solid, liquid, or gas

mixture—composition of two or more substances that are not chemically bonded and are capable of being separated

molecule—smallest particle of a substance that retains its properties

neutron—particle with no charge found inside the nucleus of an atom

nucleus—small, dense part in the middle of an atom, containing protons and neutrons

particle—very small part

periodic table—table showing all of the elements and how they are grouped

properties—qualities that make each element unique

proton—particle with a positive charge found inside the nucleus of an atom

quantum—smallest amount of energy that can exist independently

reactive—substance that easily combines with other substances in chemical reactions

state of matter—one of three forms that matter can take—either liquid, gas, or solid

Chemistry Through Time

600 B.C. Thales of Miletus (Turkey), founder of the Ionion school of natural philosophy, asserts that matter exists in three forms: mist, water, and earth

430 B.C. Democritus of Abdera (Greece), expands the concept of atoms, asserting that they explain the nature of all matter

340 B.C. Aristotle teaches that space is always filled with matter, and the four elements—earth, water, air, and fire—undergo change when combined

100 A.D. Hero of Alexandria (Egypt) shows that air expands when heated

400 The term *chemistry* is used for the first time by Alexandrian scholars to describe the activity of changing matter

1597 Andreas Libavius of Saxony, Germany, writes one of the first important chemistry textbooks, *Alchemia*

1620 Flemish scientist Johannes van Helmont uses the word *gas* to describe substances such as air

1661 Robert Boyle refutes Aristotle's ideas on the chemical composition of matter in *The Sceptical Chymist*, introducing the concepts of elements, alkalis, and acids

1766 English chemist Henry Cavendish discovers hydrogen, which he calls inflammable air

1778 Antoine Lavoisier suggests that air is made of two gases (oxygen and nitrogen)

1779 Lavoisier proposes the name oxygen for the component of air that is breathable by living organisms and responsible for combustion

1781	Joseph Priestley ignites hydrogen in oxygen, producing water
1803	John Dalton formulates his atomic theory of matter
1860	Gustav Kirchhoff and Robert Bunsen use a spectroscope to identify an element for the first time and name it cesium
1863	English chemist John Newlands develops the law of octaves, an early version of the periodic table
1869	Russian chemist Dmitri Mendeleev publishes the first version of the periodic table of the elements
1930	Electrophoresis is introduced by Swedish chemist Arne Tiselius as a way to separate proteins in suspension using electric currents
1940	The first element is created with an atomic number higher than uranium (element 93, neptunium) by Americans Philip Abelson and Edwin McMillan; carbon-14 is discovered by Canadian-American biochemist Martin Kamen
1941	American Glenn Seaborg and co-workers create plutonium (element 94) and later create atomic numbers 95, 96, and 99
1982	A single atom of element 109 is produced in a German laboratory
1988	Chemists estimate that 10 million specific compounds are recorded, with 400,000 more described each year
2008	Scientists create graphene, the world's thinnest membrane, made of a single layer of carbon atoms

Robert Boyle (1627–1691)
Irish chemist and physicist who explored the characteristics
of gases and developed the law that bears his name,
Boyle's law

Robert Wilhelm Bunsen (1811–1899)
German chemist who worked on methods to identify,
separate, and measure quantities of inorganic substances;
also invented many pieces of laboratory equipment, including
the spectroscope and an electrochemical battery; though the
Bunsen burner is named after him, his technician, C. Desaga,
is thought to have developed it

Henry Cavendish (1731–1810)
English chemist and physicist who discovered hydrogen and
determined the mass of Earth

Marie Sklodowska-Curie (1867–1934)
Polish-born French chemist, who, with her husband,
Pierre Curie, isolated the radioactive elements radium and
polonium; the first person to win two Nobel Prizes (1903
and 1911); the element curium is named after her

John Dalton (1766–1844)
British chemist and physicist who, as a student of weather
and the nature of gases, determined Dalton's law of partial
pressures and an atomic theory of matter

Sir Humphrey Davy (1778–1829)
British chemist who established the important connection
between electrochemistry and the elements

Josiah Willard Gibbs (1839–1903)
American mathematician and theoretical physicist and
chemist who applied the principles of thermodynamics
to chemistry

Otto Hahn (1879–1968)
German chemist and discoverer of element 105, unnilpentium; discovered the process of fission of heavy nuclei, which led to the development of the atomic bomb

Antoine Laurent Lavoisier (1743–1794)
French chemist who determined the nature of combustion; stated the law of conservation of matter and wrote the first modern chemistry book

Dmitri Ivanovich Mendeleev (1834–1907)
Russian chemist who published the first periodic table of the elements in 1869, leaving gaps in the table for elements then unknown; later, element 101, mendelevium, is named after him

Alfred Bernhard Nobel (1833–1896)
Swedish chemist, engineer, and inventor who discovered the element nobelium; credited as the inventor of dynamite and several other explosives; instituted the Nobel Prize

Linus Carl Pauling (1901–1994)
American chemist who applied quantum theory to molecular structures, establishing modern theoretical organic chemistry; determined the role of electrons in the formation of molecules and developed theories on ionic and covalent bonding

Joseph Louis Proust (1754–1826)
French chemist who worked to measure the mass of each component of a compound; formulated the law of definite proportions, which states that compounds always contain certain elements in the same proportion

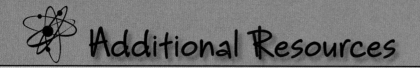

Gore, Bryson. *Physics: A Hair Is Wider Than a Million Atoms*. Mankato, Minn.: Stargazer Books, 2006.

Cooper, Sharon Katz. *The Periodic Table: Mapping the Elements*. Minneapolis: Compass Point Books, 2007.

Juettner, Bonnie. *Molecules*. Farmington Hills, Mich.: Kidhaven Press, 2005.

Solway, Andrew. *A History of Super Science*. Chicago: Raintree, 2006.

Stewart, Melissa. *Atoms*. Minneapolis: Compass Point Books, 2003.

Stille, Darlene R. *Atoms & Molecules: Building Blocks of the Universe*. Minneapolis: Compass Point Books, 2007.

Woodford, Chris, and Martin Clowes. *Atoms and Molecules*. San Diego: Blackbirch Press, 2004.

On the Web

For more information on this topic, use FactHound.

1. Go to *www.facthound.com*
2. Choose your grade level.
3. Begin your search.

This book's ID number is 9780756540692

FactHound will find the best sites for you.

Index

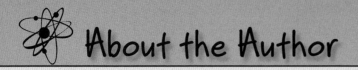

Jane Weir

Jane Weir grew up in Leicester, England. She graduated from the University of Sheffield with a master's degree in physics and astronomy, but gained much of her practical knowledge of physics through rock-climbing. Weir currently lives in Salisbury, England, where she works as a scientist for the British government.

Image Credits